The Adventures of Largo & Shelby

By Joanne Randall

Illustrated by Jason D. McIntosh

First Printing, 2018

ISBN 9780692086339

www.LeapYearMarketing.com/Largo

Largo decided to start heading home.
The sun was down past the tall trees.

Largo was a little sad to leave the playground
before everyone else, but he knew it took
longer for him to get home.

He was a turtle, after all.

Walking home was always a little lonely. Largo tried to be happy, but sometimes he wondered why he was so different from his friends.

Being a turtle made him miss out on the last few minutes of play time. It made him late to school and dinner sometimes. No matter how hard he tried, or how badly he wanted to go faster, he just couldn't.

He was a turtle, and that was that.

When Largo had walked about halfway home,
he heard his friends coming up behind him.

As usual, Jack Rabbit was first.
"Hi Largo! See you tomorrow!"

"Wait!" Largo shouted after
Jack Rabbit. "Would you walk
with me the rest of the way home?"

Largo kept walking.

Along the path came Eliza Snake.
"Excuse me, Largo. Need to get through."

"Wait!" said Largo. "Would you walk, I mean, slither, with me the rest of the way home, Eliza?"

"Sorry, Largo. My mom needs my help watching little Monty while she makes dinner."

And off she went.

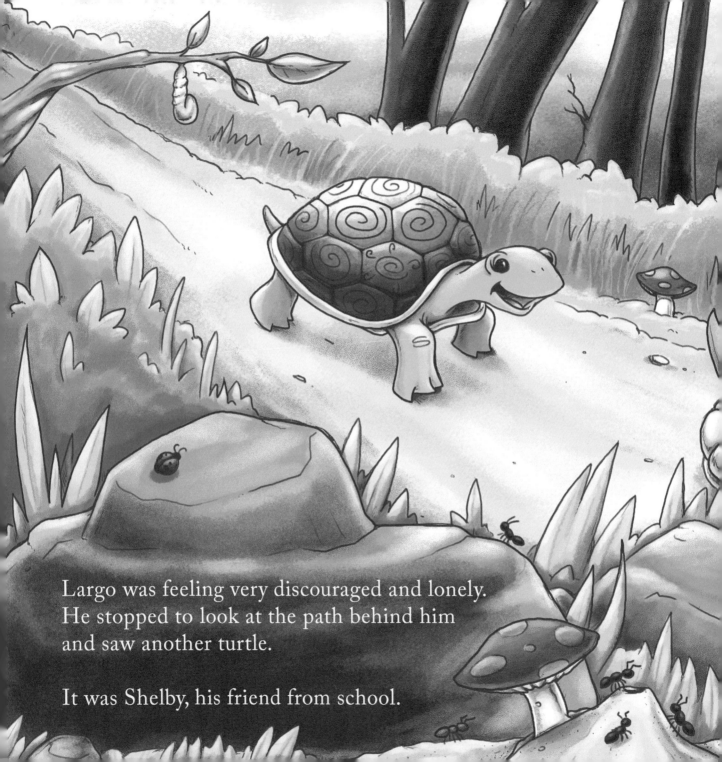

Largo was feeling very discouraged and lonely. He stopped to look at the path behind him and saw another turtle.

It was Shelby, his friend from school.

"Largo, will you walk the rest of the way home with me?

No one wants to be late so I have been walking home all by myself."

"I would love to walk home with you, Shelby. I know how you feel. Sometimes I feel sad because I can't keep up with everyone."

"I think," said Largo, "that there must be a reason why we were made this way."

"There must be," said Shelby, "although it is hard to understand."

"You're a good friend, Shelby," said Largo.

"You too," said Shelby.

Most of the remainder of the walk home was quiet. Once in a while, Shelby or Largo would comment about the birds or the trees, sometimes making a little joke.

"I am glad we walked together.
This was very nice. Thank you, Largo."

"You're welcome. Thank you, too."

As Largo and Shelby climbed over the last hill before reaching their houses, they came upon the most beautiful sunset either one of them had seen in their entire turtle lives.

"Oh, Shelby! Now I understand why we were made to be slow. We were meant to see this special sunset. If we had hurried into our houses like the others we would have missed it!"

Shelby smiled at Largo. "Yes. It all makes sense now."

Shelby and Largo smiled at each other and waved goodbye. Largo was as happy as a turtle could be.

He was special and could do things that others couldn't because he was made to be slow.

How funny was that! It made Largo laugh out loud.

(Or is it the beginning?)

CPSIA information can be obtained
at www.ICGtesting.com
Printed in the USA
LVRC021719261119
638480LV00001B/1

* 9 7 8 0 6 9 2 0 8 6 3 3 9 *